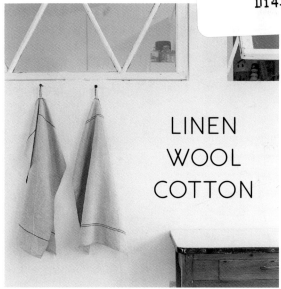

LINEN
WOOL
COTTON

# LINEN
# WOOL
# COTTON

----------

## 25 SIMPLE PROJECTS
## TO SEW WITH
## NATURAL FABRICS

AKIKO MANO

TRUMPETER
Boston & London
2009

# CONTENTS

6  *Introduction*

## LINEN

12  Sarong Apron
14  Handkerchief
18  Slouch Bag
22  Hand Towel
24  Wastebasket Cover
28  Duvet Cover
32  Pillowcases
34  Dish Towels
38  Fruit Bag
42  Apron
46  *Essay: Why I'm Attracted to Antiques*

## WOOL

52 Muffler
53 Socks
56 Mary Jane Slippers
62 Blanket
64 Hot Water Bottle Cover
68 Lap Blanket
70 Messenger Bag
72 *Essay: White, Undyed, and Stamped*

## COTTON

78 Jumper
84 Hanging Pockets
86 Floor Mat
87 Small Bag
90 Sweets Mat
94 Lingerie Case
96 Lunch Bag
100 Parent's and Child's Bags
104 *Essay: Inspiration from Foreign Books*

106 *How to Cross-Stitch*
108 *Notes on Sewing*
111 *Resources*

NOTES:

A couple of conventions are observed throughout this book:

- Dimensions are expressed in terms of width × length.
- Unless the instructions specify handwork, everything should be sewn by machine.

# INTRODUCTION

Having been born and raised in a family of clothing manufacturers, I was always surrounded by fabric, thread, and sewing machines. From early childhood, I imitated my parents by making clothes for my stuffed animals, and when I grew up, I wanted to create things for my own child. It was during this time that I decided to investigate all kinds of material and went to visit a neighborhood that was home to several textile wholesalers. The sight of all those fabrics—many of which I'd never seen before—all piled up in one place was thrilling. My dreams became more expansive, and I wondered if I could make this or accomplish that given a specific kind of cloth.

I also learned that fabrics made from the same raw materials can differ greatly in appearance—due to the threads and weaves employed—as well as in texture, wrinkle resistance, color gradations, and other individual characteristics. As I handle each fabric, I try to think of what the most suitable use for it might be. I'm pleased when I can find that use, when I can make something without changing the nuances of the cloth even if I change its form, when the essential nature of the material remains.

As I browse through fabric stores, I occasionally feel an irresistible attraction to a certain one, something akin to love at first sight. In this book, I have taken the fabrics that appeal to me in this way and used them in projects that please me.

Many people helped me put this book together. I'll be delighted if those of you who read it find it to be a source of pleasure.

—AKIKO MANO

# LINEN

With its texture and color, its detailed weave, and its softness, linen is one of my favorite textiles. It makes me want to use it for everything in my home.

The term *linen* truly covers a wide variety of textiles: everything from rough, resilient, rustic-looking fabrics to finely woven, supple material with a luxurious texture.

Pure white linen connotes cleanliness, is smooth and silky to the touch, and is simply pleasant to have around. As such, it is perfectly suited for bedding, including pillowcases and duvet covers. The indescribable feeling you get when linen brushes against your cheek is unique, which is why linen pillowcases are one of my favorite things to make.

I like the natural color of unbleached linen for dish towels and aprons. In fact, the first linen item I ever made was an apron.

Starch works well on this fabric, and the texture of well-starched, resilient linen changes as it is laundered over time. I enjoy watching these changes as an item becomes more and more a part of my everyday life. With its superb durability, linen is a reliable fabric for items that you intend to use for a long time.

# SARONG APRON

Instructions on page 12

# SARONG APRON

The way the fabric is gathered changes the silhouette of the apron. If you pull the gathers at the middle tight and loosen them at either end, you reduce the total volume of the apron and prevent the look from becoming too cutesy.

## FINISHED MEASUREMENTS

25¼" waist × 30½" long

## MATERIALS

- Linen: 42⅛" × 26"
- Embroidery floss: Red

## INSTRUCTIONS

❶ For each of the two ties, fold the long edges ⅜" to the wrong side and press. Fold one short edge ⅜" to the wrong side and press again. Fold the fabric in half lengthwise, wrong sides together, and edgestitch along the three folded sides.

❷ Fold the fabric for the waistband in half lengthwise, right sides together. Insert a tie in either end, aligning the raw edges of each tie with the raw edges of the waistband. Sew the ties in place ⅜" from the edge of the

## CUTTING THE FABRIC

Dimensions include the seam allowance. All seam allowances are ⅜" unless otherwise indicated in parentheses.

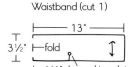

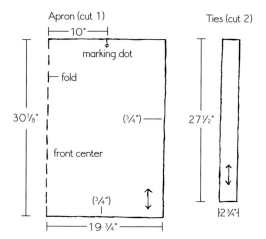

fabric, stopping ⅜" from the bottom edge of the waistband.

❸ Turn the waistband right side out.

❹ Embroider the waistband as desired.

❺ Fold the long edges of the apron fabric ⅜" to the wrong side and press. Fold one short edge ⅜" to the wrong side and press again. Fold each of the three sides under ⅜" again, press, and stitch in place.

❻ Make gathers (see page 110) on the top,

raw edge of the apron. Using the marking dot as a guide, lay the right side of the waistband against the wrong side of the apron, aligning the raw edges. Sew one layer of the waistband fabric to the apron, ⅜" from the edge.

❼ Fold the waistband toward the apron front. Fold the raw edges of the waistband ⅜" to the wrong side and press. Edgestitch along all four sides of the waistband.

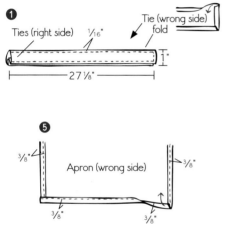

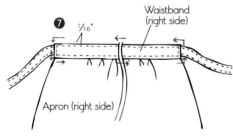

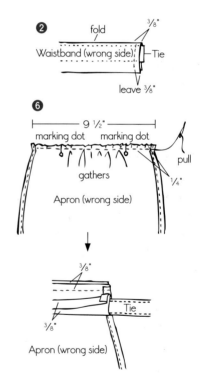

# HANDKERCHIEF

The embroidery shown here is based on some antique cross-stitch I found in a flea market. I couldn't forget the pattern, so I modified it a bit and embroidered it on a handkerchief.

## FINISHED MEASUREMENTS

13¾" × 13¾"

## MATERIALS

Linen: 15" × 15"
Embroidery floss: Navy blue

## INSTRUCTIONS

❶ Hemstitch the handkerchief (see instructions on the opposite page) and embroider as desired.

❷ Fold each edge ¼" to the wrong side and press. Fold each edge under ⅜" again, press, and edgestitch in place.

## CUTTING THE FABRIC

Dimensions include the seam allowance. All seam allowances are indicated in parentheses.

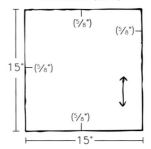

Handkerchief (cut 1)

(⅝")
(⅝")
15"
(⅝")
(⅝")
15"

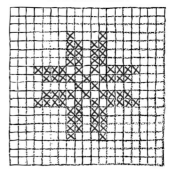

Cross-Stitch Pattern

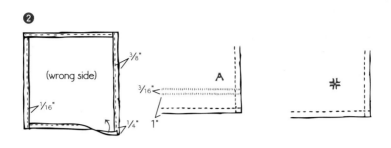

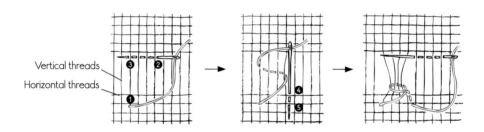

Vertical threads

Horizontal threads

## HEMSTITCH

Pull out one or more horizontal threads (see page 108). Using a needle threaded with one strand of thread the same color as the fabric, pick up four vertical threads by inserting your needle from right to the left (❶–❸). Loop the thread over the four threads you picked up, pick up two horizontal threads the right of the hemstitch (❹–❺) and gently pull. Repeat steps ❶ through ❺.

# HANDKERCHIEF

Instructions on page 14

# SLOUCH BAG
Instructions on page 18

# SLOUCH BAG

I fell in love with the color of this material the first time I saw it, and I instantly wanted to use it for a large, carryall bag. This kind of sudden encounter is part of the joy of looking at fabrics.

## FINISHED MEASUREMENTS

23¾" × 21¼"
(The handle should be long enough to let you use this as a shoulder bag if you're wearing lightweight clothing.)

## MATERIALS

Linen: 54⅓" × 26"
Sewing machine thread: Green

## INSTRUCTIONS

❶ Make gathers (see page 110) along the top edges of the two bag pieces and tighten them to 6¹¹⁄₁₆".

❷ Edgestitch around the three raw edges of each bag piece to prevent fraying.

❸ Place the front of the bag on the back of the bag, right sides together. Align the edges and sew ⅜" from the edge around the sides and bottom, starting and finishing 4¾" from the

## CUTTING THE FABRIC

Dimensions include the seam allowance. All seam allowances are ⅜".

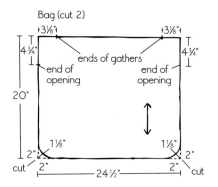

Bag (cut 2)

Top Band (cut 4)

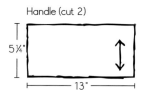

Handle (cut 2)

top edge and backstitching at the beginning and end. Finish the sides of the bag opening by pressing open the seam allowance and folding the raw edges to the wrong side. Stitch in place. Backstitch across the bottom of the opening with green thread.

❹ Place the top bands right sides together. Lay them on the right side of the bag front, aligning the top edges. Sew the three layers together ⅜" from the edge. Repeat for the back of the bag.

❺ Fold each piece of the handle in half lengthwise, right sides together. Sew

⅜" along the long raw edge and turn right side out.

❻ Insert the handle between the top bands, aligning the outer sides of the handle ⅜" from the outer sides of the bag. Sew ⅜" from the edge along top edge to secure the handle in place and ⅜" from the edge along the sides to close the top band. Turn the band right side out. Repeat for the back of the bag.

❼ Fold the bottom edges of the top bands under ⅜" and sew. Stitch three horizontal lines along the bottom of the top band with green thread.

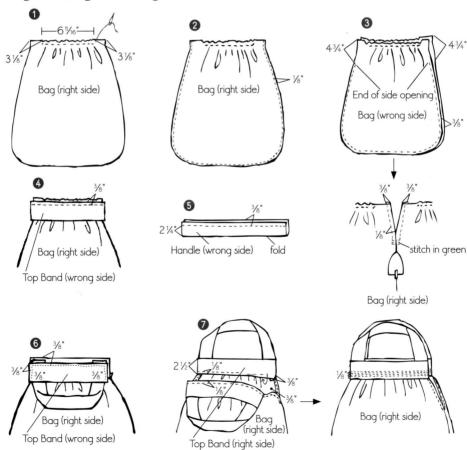

# HAND TOWEL

Instructions on page 22

# WASTEBASKET COVER

Instructions on page 24

# HAND TOWEL

Linen towels dry quickly and feel better on your skin each time you use them. The ruffle adds extra charm.

## FINISHED MEASUREMENTS

13⅜" × 35½"

## MATERIAL

Linen: 27½" × 38⅛"

## INSTRUCTIONS

❶ Take the towel fabric and fold the top edge and the side without selvage ⅜" to the wrong side; press. Fold under another ⅜", press again, and edge stitch.

❷ Edgestitch along the bottom of the ruffle fabric to prevent fraying. Fold the short end without the selvage ⅜" to the wrong side and press. Fold under another ⅜", press again, and edgestitch.

❸ Make gathers (see page 110) along the top edge of the ruffle. Pull the gathers until the ruffle is the same width as the towel.

❹ Place the ruffle on the towel, right sides together, and align the raw

## CUTTING THE FABRIC

Dimensions include the seam allowance. All seam allowances are ⅜" unless otherwise indicated in parentheses.

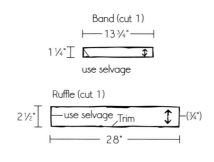

Band (cut 1)
├─── 13¾" ───┤
1¼" ⊺
use selvage

Ruffle (cut 1)
2½" ⊺  ─use selvage  Trim  ↕ ─(¾")
├──── 28" ────┤

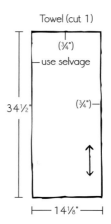

Towel (cut 1)
(¾")
─use selvage
(¾")─
34½"

├─ 14⅛" ─┤

edges. Place the band on the ruffle, wrong side up, and align the raw edges. Sew ⅜" from the edge through all three layers. Trim the seam allowance, leaving ¼".

❺ Fold the top and sides of the band ⅜" to the wrong side. Press and edgestitch along all three sides, securing the band to the towel and covering the seam.

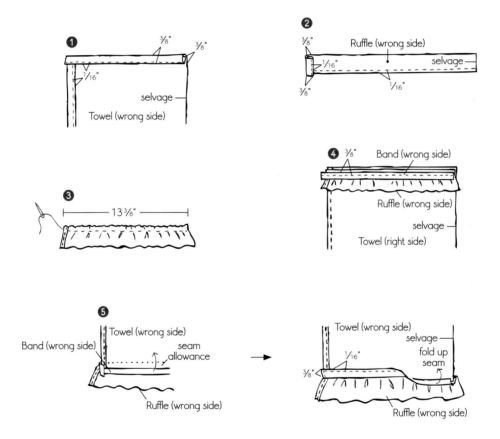

# WASTEBASKET COVER

I could never find any wastebaskets that I liked for my home. I kept practical considerations in mind for this cover, so it can hold a trash bag.

## FINISHED MEASUREMENTS

11¾" × 16¾" × 6"

## MATERIALS

Linen (sailcloth): 19" × 42½"
Cotton: 14⅛" × 21½"
Cotton tape (¾" wide): 3⅛", 2 strips
Snaps (⅜" in diameter): 2

## INSTRUCTIONS

❶ Fold each handle piece in half lengthwise, right sides together. Sew ⅜" from the edge along two sides. Turn the handles right side out.

❷ Fold the bag piece in half, wrong sides together, and align the edges. Sew ³⁄₁₆" from the edge along both sides. Turn the bag inside out and sew ⅜"from the seams on both sides.

❸ Make a gusset in the bottom of the bag by folding the corners up 1¼" and stitching them to the side seam allowance.

## CUTTING THE FABRIC

Dimensions include the seam allowance. All seam allowances are ⅜" unless otherwise indicated in parentheses.

Bag (linen sailcloth) (cut 1)

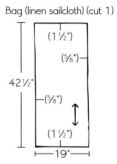

Handle (cotton) (cut 2)

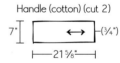

④ Fold the top edge of the bag ⅜" to the wrong side and press. Fold under another 1¼" and press again.

⑤ Unfold the top edge once. Locate the middle front and middle back just below the first top crease on the outside of the bag and mark with a dot. Attach one snap gusset to each dot.

⑥ Fold the top edge down again along the crease. Insert one end of a cotton tape strip in the fold just under each snap and sew in place. Insert the unsewn end of a handle in the fold at each side seam and sew in place. Fold the ends of the cotton tape over twice and blind stitch; attach a snap ball to the outside of each tape strip. Lay out the handles so they trail away from the bag and sew ³⁄₁₆" from the top edge for reinforcement. Turn the bag right side out.

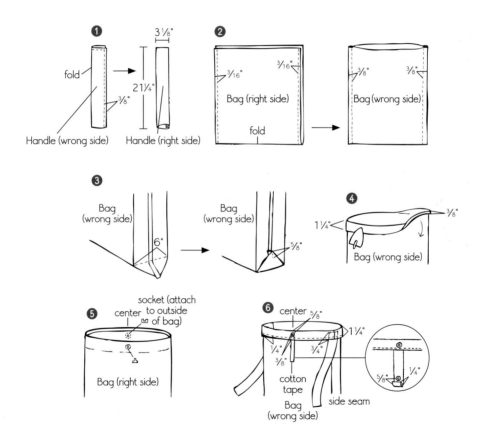

# DUVET COVER

Instructions on page 28

# DUVET COVER

This a great cover for a small duvet. You join three panels and sew them up with red thread. Using somewhat thicker fabric will make the cover even more durable. (Note: The finished size is slightly smaller than a standard twin-size duvet.)

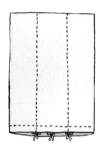

## FINISHED MEASUREMENTS

59⅛" × 82⅜"

## MATERIALS

Linen: 59⅞" with selvage × 259⅞"
Sewing machine thread: Red

## INSTRUCTIONS

❶ Fold the long edges of the outer tab ⅜" to the wrong side and press. Fold one short edge ⅜" to the wrong side and press. Fold the fabric in half lengthwise, wrong sides together, and edgestitch along the three open sides. Fold the long edges of the inner tab ⁵⁄₁₆" to the wrong side and press. Fold the short edges ⅜" to the wrong side and press. Fold the fabric in half lengthwise, wrong sides together, and edgestitch along the three open sides.

❷ To make the front of the cover, place one side panel on the central panel, right sides together, and align the left sides. Place the other side panel, on top

## CUTTING THE FABRIC

Dimensions include the seam allowance. All seam allowances are ⅜" unless otherwise indicated in parentheses.

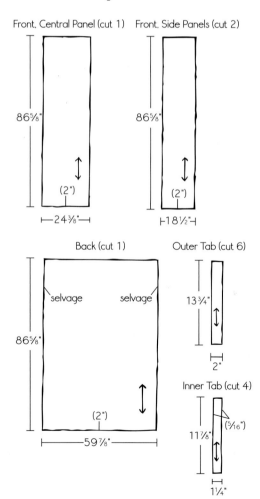

of the first two pieces, wrong side up, and align the right side with the right side of the central panel. Sew ⅜" from the edge along both sides. Finish the seams with a zigzag stitch or lockstitch. Press the seam allowance toward the center and topstitch the center panel ³⁄₁₆" from the seam with red thread.

❸ Place the front cover on the back cover, right sides together, and align the edges. Sew ⅜" from the edge along the top edge and both sides. Beginning 2" from the bottom edge, sew 11½" in from either side, leaving an opening. Finish all the seams except

those near the opening with a zigzag stitch or lockstitch.

❹ Fold the bottom edge ⅜" to the wrong side and press. Fold under another 1½" and press.

❺ Insert three outer tabs in the fold on both sides of the opening. Edgestitch along the bottom hem, securing the outer tabs in place. Reinforce the ends of the opening by backstitching with red thread.

❻ Sew the four inside tabs to the seam allowance ⅜" from the edge at each corner, as shown in the diagram. Turn the cover right side out.

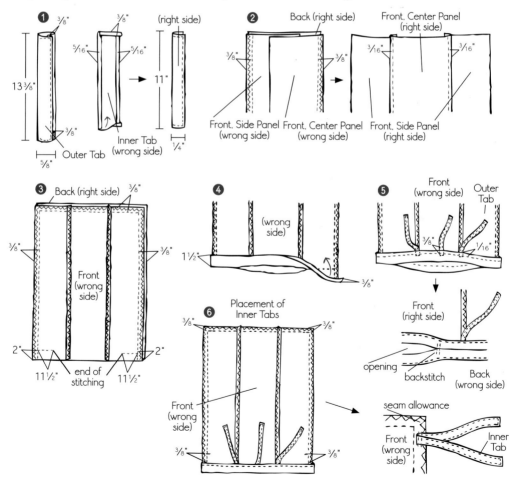

# PILLOWCASES

Instructions on page 32

# PILLOWCASES

I like the clean, fresh look of pure white pillowcases. The linen used for these cases feels so good against your skin that once you try them, you'll be hooked.

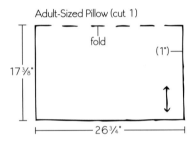

## FINISHED MEASUREMENTS

Adult size: 25⅜" × 17"
Child size: 15⅛" × 10⅝"
Adjust all measurements as necessary to fit your pillow forms.

## MATERIALS

Linen
  Adult size: 26¾" × 34¾"
  Child size: 16½" × 22"
Embroidery floss: Red
Buttons (⅜" in diameter)
  Adult size: 3 buttons
  Child size: 2 buttons

## INSTRUCTIONS

❶ Embroider a monogram on the front of the pillowcase if desired (see page 106).

❷ Fold the fabric in half, right sides together, and sew ⅜" from the edge on two sides, leaving an opening on one short side. Finish the seams with a

## CUTTING THE FABRIC

Dimensions include the seam allowance. All seam allowances are ⅜" unless otherwise indicated in parentheses.

Adult-Sized Pillow (cut 1)

17⅜"

fold

(1")

26¾"

Child-Sized Pillow (cut 1)

11"

fold    (1")

16½"

zigzag stitch or lockstitch. Turn the pillowcase right side out.

❸ Fold the open edge ⅜" to the wrong side and press. Fold under another ⅝", press again, and edgestitch.

❹ Sew the buttons on (3 for the adult-sized pillow, 2 for the child-sized pillow) at equal intervals along one side of the opening. Make corresponding buttonholes along the opposite side of the opening, following the instructions for your sewing machine.

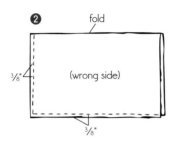

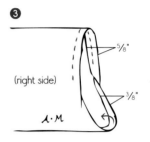

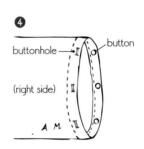

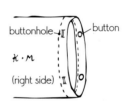

# DISH TOWELS

I really like fabric with a pattern to it. I use the zigzag function on my sewing machine to make the simple lines in these dish towels.

## FINISHED MEASUREMENTS

19⅜" × 26⅞"

## MATERIALS

Linen: 20⅞" × 30⅜"
Sewing machine thread: Black or red

## INSTRUCTIONS

❶ Fold the long edges of the tab ⅜" to the wrong side and press. Fold the tab in half lengthwise, wrong sides together, and edgestitch.

❷ Create two or four decorative bands across the towel, using a ¹⁄₁₆" zigzag stitch. Place bands approximately 4" from the top and bottom edges.

❸ Fold the side edges and bottom edge of the towel ⅜" to the wrong side and press. Fold under another ⅜" and press again. Fold the top edge of the towel over ¼" to the wrong side and press. Fold under another ⅜" and press again. Fold the tab in half and insert the ends in the fold at the middle of the top edge. Edgestitch along all four sides of the towel.

## CUTTING THE FABRIC

Dimensions include the seam allowance. All seam allowances are ⅜" unless otherwise indicated in parentheses.

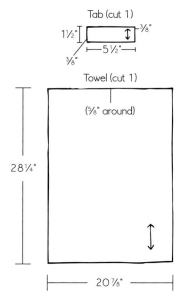

Tab (cut 1)

1½"  ⅜"
⅜"  5½"

Towel (cut 1)

(⅝" around)

28¼"

20⅞"

**❶**

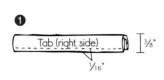

Tab (right side)

$\frac{3}{8}$"

$\frac{1}{16}$"

**❷** Towel with two stripes

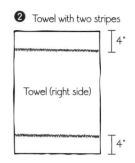

Towel (right side)

4"

4"

**❸**

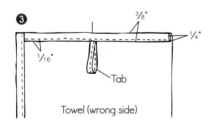

$\frac{3}{8}$"

$\frac{1}{4}$"

$\frac{1}{16}$"

Tab

Towel (wrong side)

Towel with four stripes

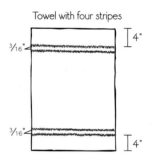

4"

$\frac{3}{16}$"

$\frac{3}{16}$"

4"

# DISH TOWELS

Instructions on page 34

# FRUIT BAG

Instructions on page 38

# FRUIT BAG

I used cheesecloth, very lightweight cotton gauze, for this nearly transparent bag. You can store lemons, oranges, or apples in it and hang it from a hook to add a touch of charm to your kitchen.

## FINISHED MEASUREMENTS

7⅞" × 9⅞"

## MATERIALS

Cheesecloth: 17⅜" × 10¼"
Linen: 23⅝" × 23⅝"

## INSTRUCTIONS

❶ Place the front piece on the back piece, right sides together. If you like, place a decorative tag between the two layers, aligning the raw edges. Sew ⅜" from the edge along the sides and bottom. Finish the seam with a zigzag stitch or lockstitch. Turn the bag right side out.

❷ Make the linen bias tape by folding a strip of linen in half lengthwise and press. Open, fold both edges to the center crease, and press. Cut two pieces of bias tape to the length of the top middle of the bag. Fold the bias tape over the top middle of the

## CUTTING THE FABRIC

Dimensions include the seam allowance. All seam allowances are ⅜" unless otherwise indicated in parentheses.

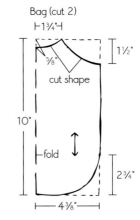

Bag (cut 2)

1¾"

⅝"

cut shape

1½"

10"

fold

2¾"

4⅜"

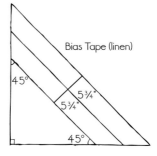

Bias Tape (linen)

45°

5¾"

5¾"

45°

bag front and back and edgestitch in place.

❸ Cut a length of bias tape long enough to cover the top sides of the bag, make two 8¼" handles, and provide ⅜" for a seam allowance. Place the ends of the bias tape with right sides together and sew ⅜" from the edge, making a circle. Fold the bias tape over the sides of the bag opening, leaving the extra tape loose to serve as handles. Edgestitch the length of the bias tape, securing it in place and finishing the handle.

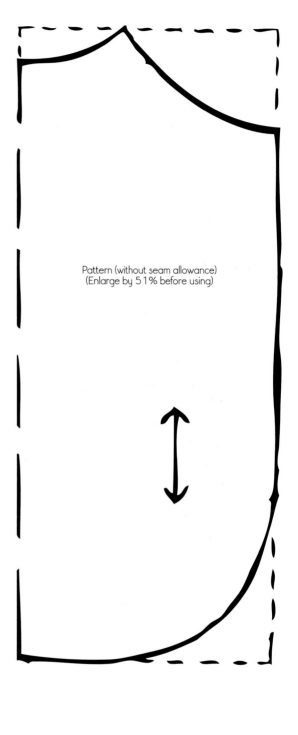

Pattern (without seam allowance)
(Enlarge by 51% before using)

❶

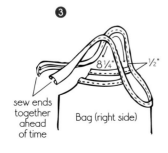

Bag (right side)

Bag (wrong side)

Tag

❷

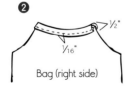

½"

⅟₁₆"

Bag (right side)

❸

8¼

½"

sew ends together ahead of time

Bag (right side)

# APRON

Instructions on page 42

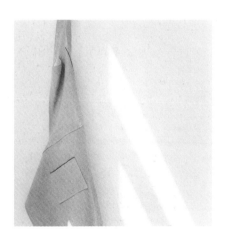

# APRON

If you fold the bib on this long, low-waisted apron down and back, you can turn it into a sarong style.

## FINISHED MEASUREMENTS

28" × 31½" for the skirt portion

## MATERIALS

Linen: 59" × 32⅝"
Sewing machine thread: Red

## INSTRUCTIONS

❶ Fold one long edge of the pocket ⅜" to the wrong side and press. Fold under another ¾", press again, and edgestitch.

❷ Fold the long edges of the neck strap ⅜" to the wrong side and press. Fold the fabric in half lengthwise, wrong sides together, and sew ³⁄₁₆" from the edge along the two long sides.

❸ Fold the long edges of both ties ⅜" to the wrong side and press. Fold one short edge on each ⅜" to the wrong side and press. Fold each tie in half lengthwise, wrong sides together, and sew ³⁄₁₆" from the edge along the three pressed sides.

## CUTTING THE FABRIC

Dimensions include the seam allowance. All seam allowances are ⅜" unless otherwise indicated in parentheses.

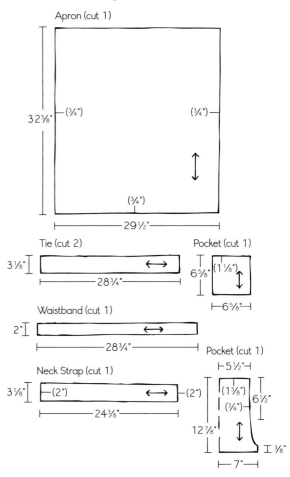

❹ Make a decorative zigzag stitch in red down the length of the bib approximately 2¾" from the right edge and along the top edge of the pocket.

❺ Fold the side edges of the bib ⅜" to the wrong side and press. Fold under another ⅜" and press again. Fold the top edge ⅜" to the wrong side and press. Fold under another 1" and press again. Open the folds and cut the corners as shown and refold the sides. Place the bib right side up. Refold the top edge along the crease to the wrong side.

❻ Lay the bib wrong side up. Insert the ends of the neck strap in the fold along the top of the bib, aligning the sides. Edgestitch in place.

❼ Fold the neck strap up and sew it to the upper edge of the bib. Edgestitch both sides of the bib.

❽ Fold the side edges of the apron ⅜" (to the wrong side and press. Fold under another ⅜" and press again. Fold the bottom edge ⅜" to the wrong side and press. Fold under another ⅜" and

press again. Edgestitch along the bottom and both sides.

❾ Fold the side edges of the pocket ⅜" to the wrong side and press. Fold the bottom edge ⅜" to the wrong side and press. Position the pocket on the right side of the apron and sew ⁵⁄₁₆" from the edge.

❿ Place the bib on the apron, wrong sides together, and align the raw edges. Place the waistband on top of the bib, wrong side up, and align the raw edges. Sew ⅜" from the edge through all three layers.

⓫ Fold the waistband to the apron front. Fold the long edge of the waistband ⅜" to the wrong side and press. Sew ³⁄₁₆" from the edge, securing the waistband to the apron front. Insert the end of a tie ⅜" into each side of the waistband. Fold the side edges of the waistband to the wrong side. Sew ³⁄₁₆" from the edge along the two sides, securing the ties in place. Decorate the waistband with zigzag stitches as desired.

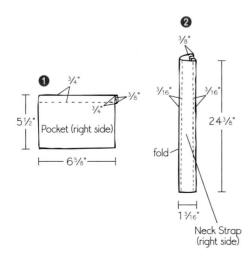

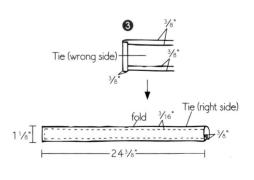

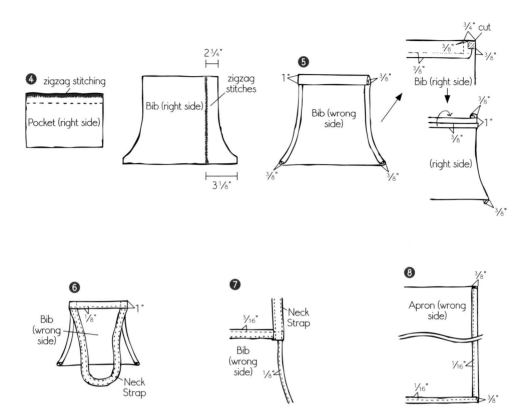

④ zigzag stitching

Pocket (right side)

2 3/4"

Bib (right side)

zigzag stitches

3 1/8"

⑤ 1"    3/8"

Bib (wrong side)

3/8"    3/8"

3/4" cut

3/8"

3/8"

3/8"    Bib (right side)

3/8"

3/8"    1"

(right side)

3/8"

⑥ 1"

1/8"

Bib (wrong side)

Neck Strap

⑦ Neck Strap

3/16"

Bib (wrong side)    1/8"

⑧ 3/8"

Apron (wrong side)

1/16"

1/16"    3/8"

44

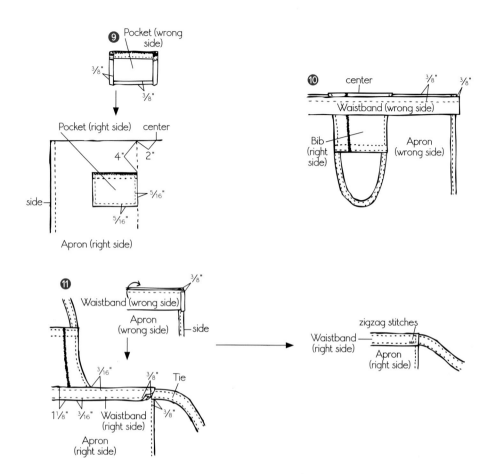

**9** Pocket (wrong side)

3/8"

3/8"

Pocket (right side)    center

4"    2"

5/16"

5/16"

side

Apron (right side)

**10** center    3/8"    3/8"

Waistband (wrong side)

Bib (right side)

Apron (wrong side)

**11** Waistband (wrong side)    3/8"

Apron (wrong side)    side

3/16"    3/8"    Tie

1 1/8"    3/16"    Waistband (right side)    3/8"

Apron (right side)

zigzag stitches

Waistband (right side)

Apron (right side)

# ESSAY
## WHY I'M ATTRACTED TO ANTIQUES

Whenever I pick up an antique, I need to mentally prepare myself for the feeling that I get from seeing its color, which has begun to fade little by little over the years, and from the dignified presence of an object that has been used and treasured over a long period of time. When I look at it, I don't want to destroy the passage of time it embodies. As with fabrics, I value chance encounters with antiques and their nuances.

I find pleasure in new items that are familiar because they are from my time period, but when I pick up an antique, I think about the person who made it and is no longer here. I imagine the process by which it has been handed down through the years, how it has passed through many people's hands without being discarded. I think of how incredibly pleased the maker of the object would be to know that it has survived for so long. The antiques I encounter as part of creating my own handiwork excite me, and I take care to create simple, well-sewn items that people won't get tired of and will use for a long time.

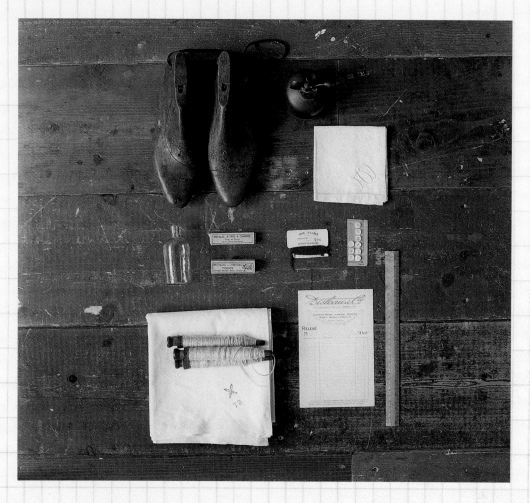

Clockwise from top left: Wooden shoe forms made in Japan; a brass atomizer (the color becomes more appealing the more I use it); a monogrammed linen handkerchief; deadstock buttons (I often use these in my creations); red embroidery thread from France; a wooden ruler from Great Britain; a notebook (I like the look of its green cover and faded colors); a bobbin that was used at an old-fashioned clothing factory in Shizuoka; military surplus cloth; a Japanese medicine bottle; yellow boxes that once contained printed ribbon.

# WOOL

Some wool fabrics have an airy, gentle feel all their own, but I prefer the thicker, fluffier varieties, which have a feeling of quality and simplicity. Wool also comes in a variety of colors so you can use it for all sorts of items.

At first glance, it may seem difficult to work with. However, most varieties are somewhat stretchable, so it's good for sewing items with curved patterns, such as Mary Jane slippers. Blankets are an obvious choice for this material and highly practical. You may want to prepare several of them for long winter evenings spent reading a book or listening to music. Socks made of silky smooth, luxurious angora make perfect winter gifts.

If you're thinking of making miscellaneous items for your home, linen and cotton are probably the first fabrics that come to mind, but wool is a material you can enjoy all year long. You just have to get acquainted with it.

# MUFFLER

Also serves as a stole
Instructions on page 52

# MUFFLER

This muffler combines two different fabrics: the side that touches your skin is double gauze, while the other side is washable linen-wool. I've added some lace and buttons as accents.

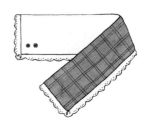

## FINISHED MEASUREMENTS

58¼" × 12¾"

## MATERIALS

Linen-wool: 59" × 13½"
Cotton: 59" × 13½"
Lace tape (2" wide): 90"
Wooden buttons (½" in diameter): 2

## INSTRUCTIONS

❶ Place the front piece on the back piece, right sides together, and align the edges. Insert the lace between the layers on both short sides and one long side, aligning the edges. Sew ⅜" from the edge along all four sides, leaving an opening of 6" along one of the long sides. Trim any excess lace.

❷ Turn the muffler right side out. Fold the edge of the opening ⅜" to the wrong side, press, and hand stitch closed. Fold over the ends of the lace and hand stitch in place.

❸ Sew buttons to the linen-wool side as shown.

## CUTTING THE FABRIC

Dimensions include the seam allowance. All seam allowances are ⅜" unless otherwise indicated in parentheses.

Front (linen-wool), Back (cotton) (cut 1 each)

13½"        59"

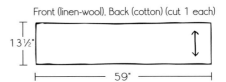

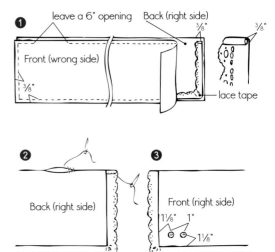

# SOCKS

You'll want to wear these cuddly socks on a cold evening. Angora wool is warm and indescribably soft. It's also stretchy, so the pattern is basically one-size-fits-all.

## FINISHED MEASUREMENTS

4" × 13⅜"

## MATERIALS

Angora wool: 17⅜" × 14½"
Elastic tape (³⁄₁₆"): approximately 25"
Buttons (⅝" in diameter): 2

## INSTRUCTIONS

❶ Fold the fabric in half lengthwise, right sides together, and sew ⅜" from the edge around the toe and up the side. Finish the seam with a zigzag stitch or lockstitch.

❷ Finish the top edge with a zigzag stitch or lockstitch. Fold the edge ¾"to the wrong side. Sew around the top ⅝" from the folded edge, leaving a small gap through which to insert the elastic tape.

❸ Insert the elastic tape in the top hem and turn the sock right side out. Sew the decorative buttons on just below the elastic casing.

## CUTTING THE FABRIC

Dimensions include the seam allowance. All seam allowances are ⅜" unless otherwise indicated in parentheses.

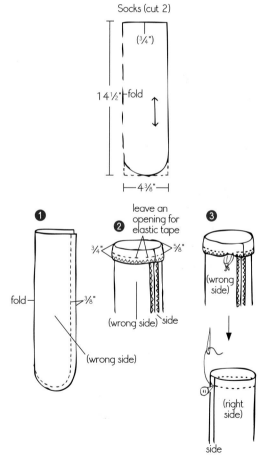

Socks (cut 2)

(¾")

14½" fold

4⅜"

❶

fold

⅜"

(wrong side)

(wrong side)

❷

leave an opening for elastic tape

¾"

⅝"

(wrong side)    side

❸

(wrong side)

(right side)

side

# SOCKS

Instructions on page 53

# MARY JANE SLIPPERS

Instructions on page 56

# MARY JANE SLIPPERS

These slippers are one of my favorite projects. Winter calls for wool, and since these slippers are lined with quilt batting, they're extra warm and snug. The soles are suede to prevent slipping.

## FINISHED MEASUREMENTS

Approximately 9" long

## MATERIALS

Wool: 31⅞" × 13⅜"
Suede: 8⅜" × 11⅛"
Cotton: 11⅞" × 12½"
Thick quilt batting: 7" × 10¼"
Velcro fasteners (½" long × ⅜" wide): 2 sets
Felt insoles (commercially available): 1 set

## INSTRUCTIONS

❶ Using pattern paper, draw and cut out the two patterns as shown under "Cutting the Fabric." (Be sure that the patterns for the right and left feet are mirror images of each other.)

❷ For each strap, fold the fabric in half lengthwise, wrong sides together, and press. Place the Velcro fastener

## CUTTING THE FABRIC

Dimensions include the seam allowance. All seam allowances are indicated in parentheses.

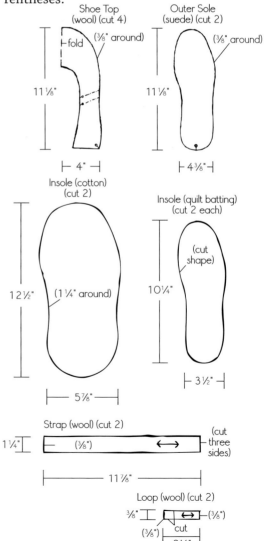

Shoe Top (wool) (cut 4)
fold
(⅜" around)
11⅛"
4"

Outer Sole (suede) (cut 2)
(⅜" around)
11⅛"
4⅜"

Insole (cotton) (cut 2)
12½"
(1¼" around)
5⅞"

Insole (quilt batting) (cut 2 each)
(cut shape)
10¼"
3½"

Strap (wool) (cut 2)
1¼"
(⅜")
(cut three sides)
11⅞"

Loop (wool) (cut 2)
⅜"
(⅜")
(⅜")
cut
2½"

on the strap as shown in the diagram. Sew ⅛" from the edge along the two long sides of the strap, securing the Velcro in place. Sew ⅜" from the edge on one short end.

❸ For each loop, fold the fabric in half lengthwise, wrong sides together, and press. Edgestitch along the long side.

❹ For each shoe, lay one shoe top right side up. Place the strap, bottom side up, and the loop on the shoe top as shown in the diagram, making sure that the loop and strap are directly across from each other and that the raw edges are aligned. Sew in place ³⁄₁₆" from the edge of the shoe top. Be sure the right and left shoes are mirror images of each other.

❺ Fold the shoe top in half, right sides together. Sew the heels ⅜" from the edge.

❻ Place the shoe top without a strap on the shoe top that has the strap, right sides together. Sew ⅜" from the edge along the top of the shoe. Cut slits in the seam allowance of the curved fabric. Turn the shoe right side out and stitch the upper edges.

❼ Align the outer sole with the shoe top, right sides together. Sew ⅜" from the edge around the sole. Cut slits in the seam allowance of the curved fabric. (Keep track of which shoe is which and make sure the strap loop is on the inside.)

❽ Make the insole. Lay the cotton insole wrong side up; center the batting on top. Place the felt insole on the batting. Fold the cotton insole over the felt insole and hand stitch in place.

❾ Place the completed insole, felt side down, on the wrong side of the outer sole. Hand stitch in place and turn the shoe right side out.

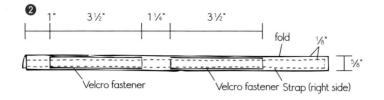

**2** | 1" | 3½" | 1¼" | 3½" | fold | ⅛"

⅝"

Velcro fastener

Velcro fastener Strap (right side)

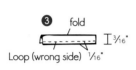

**3** fold

³/₁₆"

Loop (wrong side) ¹/₁₆"

**4** left foot

Shoe Top (right side)

Strap (wrong side)

³/₁₆"

⅜"

³/₁₆"

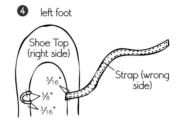

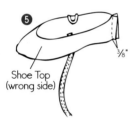

**5**

Shoe Top (wrong side)

⅜"

cut

Shoe Top (wrong side)

**6**

Shoe Top (wrong side)

⅜"

Shoe Top (right side)

Shoe Top (right side)

³/₁₆"

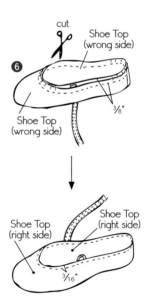

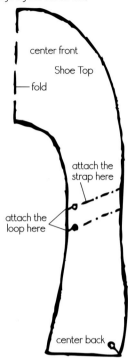

center front

Shoe Top

— fold

attach the
strap here

attach the
loop here

center back

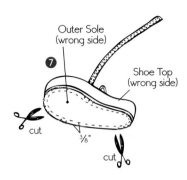

❼

Outer Sole
(wrong side)

Shoe Top
(wrong side)

cut

⅜"

cut

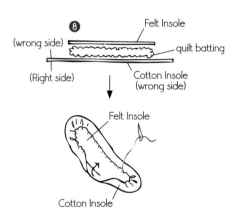

❽

Felt Insole

(wrong side)

quilt batting

(Right side)

Cotton Insole
(wrong side)

Felt Insole

Cotton Insole

Outer Sole

center back

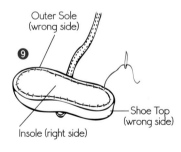

❾

Outer Sole
(wrong side)

Shoe Top
(wrong side)

Insole (right side)

59

# BLANKET

Instructions on page 62

# HOT WATER BOTTLE COVER

Instructions on page 64

# BLANKET

The front of this blanket is wool, but the backing is soft, fluffy flannel. To keep things simple, I use the same color fabric for both sides and blanket-stitch around the edges.

## FINISHED MEASUREMENTS

59" × 67"

## MATERIALS

Thick wool: 59¾" × 67¾"
Cotton flannel: 59¾" × 67¾"
Embroidery floss: Navy blue

## INSTRUCTIONS

❶ Place the front piece on the back piece, right sides together. Align the edges and sew ⅜" from the edge on all four sides, leaving a gap of 8" to 12" on one short side.

❷ Turn the blanket right side out. Fold the edge with the opening ⅜" to the wrong side and press. Hand stitch the opening closed.

❸ Blanket-stitch along the edge of the blanket to make a decorative finish.

❹ Decorate the top and bottom edges with three bullion stitches each (see opposite).

## CUTTING THE FABRIC

Dimensions include the seam allowance. All seam allowances are ⅜" unless otherwise indicated in parentheses.

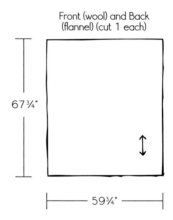

Front (wool) and Back
(flannel) (cut 1 each)

67¾"

59¾"

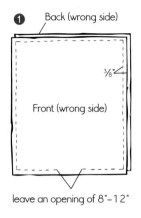

❶ Back (wrong side)

³⁄₈"

Front (wrong side)

leave an opening of 8"–12"

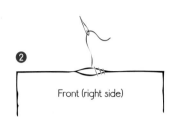

❷

Front (right side)

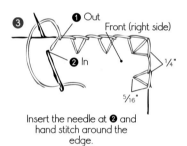

❸

❶ Out

Front (right side)

❷ In

¹⁄₄"

⁵⁄₁₆"

Insert the needle at ❷ and hand stitch around the edge.

## BULLION STITCH

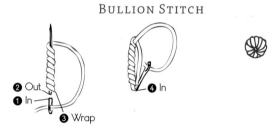

❷ Out
❶ In
❸ Wrap
❹ In

As the needle emerges from the material ❶– ❷ wrap the trailing thread around the needle about 8 times ❸, until you reach the tip. Tighten the thread and pull the needle through the fabric ❹.

# HOT WATER BOTTLE COVER

I designed this handmade cover for an old-fashioned hot water bottle. If you make it with rather thick wool, it will make the bottle just the right temperature for warming your feet on those cold winter nights.

## FINISHED MEASUREMENTS

16⅝" × 10¾" for a hot water bottle measuring 13⅛" × 10¼". Adjust all measurements as necessary to fit your hot water bottle.

## MATERIALS

Thick wool: 34¾" × 14⅛"
Flannel: 37" × 11⅞"
Rickrack (⅜" wide): 23⅝"

## INSTRUCTIONS

❶ Fold the long edges of the loop fabric 5⁄16" to the wrong side and press. Fold the fabric in half lengthwise, wrong sides together, press, and edgestitch along the long side.

❷ For ties A and B, fold the long edges ⅜" to the wrong side and press. Fold one short edge ⅜" to the wrong side

## CUTTING THE FABRIC

Dimensions include the seam allowance. All seam allowances are ⅜" unless otherwise indicated in parentheses.

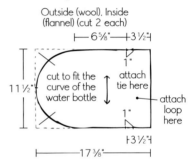

Outside (wool), Inside (flannel) (cut 2 each)

⊢—6⅝"—⊣3½⊣
1"
11½" cut to fit the curve of the water bottle / attach tie here
attach loop here
1"
⊢3½"⊣
⊢————17⅜"————⊣

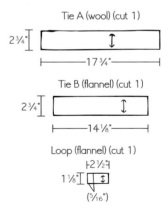

Tie A (wool) (cut 1)
2¾"⊢ ⊢————17¾"————⊣

Tie B (flannel) (cut 1)
2¾"⊢ ⊢————14⅛"————⊣

Loop (flannel) (cut 1)
⊢2½⊣
1⅛⊢
(5⁄16")

and press. Fold the tie in half lengthwise, wrong sides together, and sew ⅛" from the edge along the three pressed sides.

❸ Lay the outside bottle fabric right side up; place the loop and both ties along the edge as shown in the diagram. Sew each in place, stitching ⅛" from the edge.

❹ Lay the outside bottle fabric right side up; place the rickrack along the top, making sure the center of the rickrack is ⅜" from the edge. Repeat for the second piece of outside bottle fabric.

❺ Place the front outside fabric on the back outside, right sides together. Align the edges and sew ⅜" from the edge along the sides and bottom. Place the front lining on the back lining, right sides together. Align the edges and sew ⅜" from the edge along the sides and bottom, leaving a 4" gap on one side.

❻ Place the outside cover inside the lining, right sides together. Sew ⅜" from the edge along the top, through both layers. Turn the cover right side out and topstitch around the top edge. Fold the edges of the opening of the lining ⅜" to the wrong side, and hand stitch the opening closed.

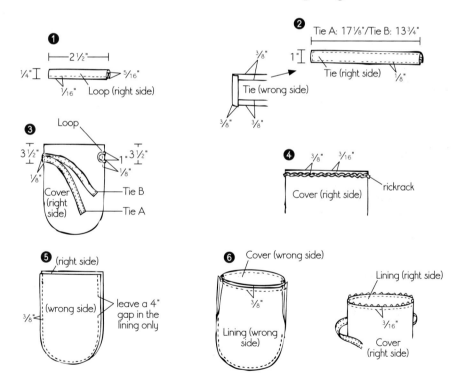

65

# LAP BLANKET

Instructions on page 68

# MESSENGER BAG

Instructions on page 70

# LAP BLANKET

You'll be happy to drape this blanket over your legs on cold winter evenings. I chose to make it with Black Watch plaid and trim both ends with ruffles.

## FINISHED MEASUREMENTS

45" × 29⅝"

## MATERIALS

Cotton: 44½" × 59⅞"
Wool: 30⅜" × 41"

## INSTRUCTIONS

❶ Fold each ruffle piece in half lengthwise, right sides together, and press. Sew ⅜" from the edge along both short ends. Turn right side out.

❷ Make gathers (see page 110) on one long side of each ruffle. Pull the gathers until the piece is 29⅝". Lay the blanket front right side up. Place one ruffle at each end, aligning the raw edges, and sew ⅜" from the edge.

❸ Place the blanket back on the blanket front, right sides together. Align the edges and sew ¾" from the edge along the short sides and ⅜" from the edge along long sides, leaving an 8" gap on one long side.

❹ Turn the blanket right side out. Fold the open edge ⅜" to the wrong side and press. Hand stitch the opening closed.

## CUTTING THE FABRIC

Dimensions include the seam allowance. All seam allowances are ⅜" unless otherwise indicated in parentheses.

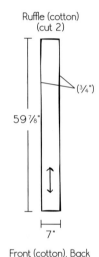

Ruffle (cotton)
(cut 2)

(¾")

59⅞"

7"

Front (cotton), Back (wool) (cut 1 each)

(¾")

41"

(¾")

30⅜"

**❶** (wrong side)     fold

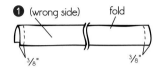

3/8"          3/8"

**❷** stitches     fold

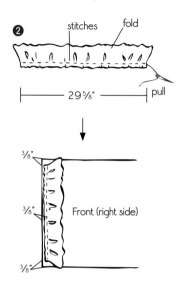

|——— 29⁵/₈" ———|  pull

⬇

3/8"

3/8"          Front (right side)

3/8"

**❸** Front (right side)     3/8"

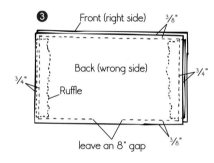

Back (wrong side)

3/4"                    3/4"

Ruffle

leave an 8" gap     3/8"

**❹**

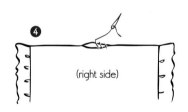

(right side)

# MESSENGER BAG

The coming of winter inspires me to use gray wool. I've added a wide band of lace for decoration, which also acts as a strap to hold down the bag flap.

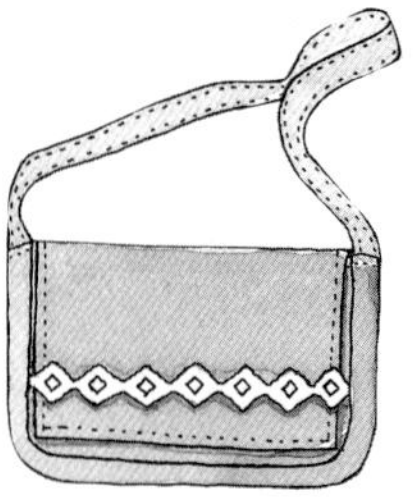

## FINISHED MEASUREMENTS

14¼" × 11⅛" × 2¾"

## MATERIALS

Thick wool: 44⅞" × 33½"
Hemp: 37" × 15⅛"
Lace (2⅜" wide): 15¾"

## INSTRUCTIONS

❶ Fold the long edges of the shoulder strap ⅜" to the wrong side and press. Fold the strap in half lengthwise, wrong sides together, and sew ⅜" from the edge along both long sides.

❷ Place the flap pieces with right sides together. Align the edges and sew ⅜" from the edge along both sides and the bottom. Turn the flap right side out and topstitch ⅜" from the edge along both sides and the bottom.

❸ Lay the front of the bag right side up. Place the lace on the fabric so that the middle of the lace is 4⅜" from the

## CUTTING THE FABRIC

Dimensions include the seam allowance. All seam allowances are ⅜" unless otherwise indicated in parentheses.

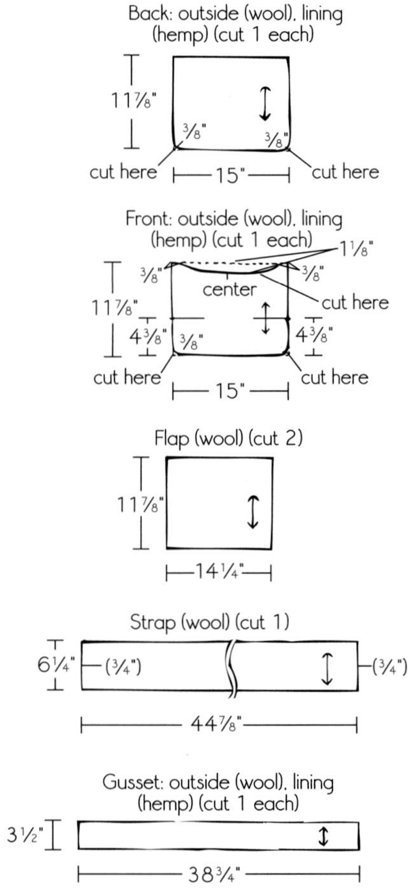
Back: outside (wool), lining (hemp) (cut 1 each)
11⅞"
⅜"
⅜"
cut here
15"
cut here
Front: outside (wool), lining (hemp) (cut 1 each)
1⅛"
⅜"
⅜"
center
cut here
11⅞"
4⅜"
⅜"
4⅜"
cut here
15"
cut here
Flap (wool) (cut 2)
11⅞"
14¼"
Strap (wool) (cut 1)
6¼"
(¾")
(¾")
44⅞"
Gusset: outside (wool), lining (hemp) (cut 1 each)
3½"
38¾"

bottom edge. Sew ³⁄₁₆" from the edge on along both sides.

❹ Place the front of the bag and the gusset with right sides together. Align the edges and sew ³⁄₈" from the edge along the sides and bottom. Repeat for the back of the bag. Turn the bag right side out. Repeat the process for the hemp lining, leaving a 6" gap along one of the sides.

❺ Place the ends of the shoulder strap along the top edges of the gusset, making sure the ends of the strap extend ³⁄₈" above the gusset edges. Place the flap on the bag back, right sides together, aligning the raw edges. Place the outer bag inside the lining, right sides together. Sew ³⁄₈" from the edge all the way around the top.

❻ Turn the bag right side out. Fold the open edge of the lining ³⁄₈" to the wrong side, press, and hand stitch closed.

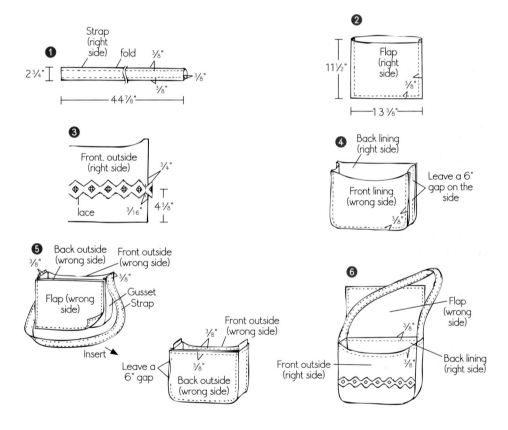

# ESSAY
## WHITE, UNDYED, AND STAMPED

When I was a child, I was always surrounded by the raw materi-als for my family's clothing factory. Even though I didn't know the names of these materials, I was always most attracted to the plain, undyed fabric that we used to wrap our finished goods—it was unbleached cotton, the sheeting used to make clothing mock-ups. Even though there must have been beauti-ful materials in every color of the rainbow lying around, I re-member the natural, unassuming ones like sheeting.

I choose my fabrics almost unconsciously and can amass quite a collection before I realize it. The linens and cottons are almost all white or undyed, yet each has its own distinct char-acteristics. There is an endless variety: herringbone, double gauze, white denim, sailcloth, organic cotton, plain-weave linen, and flannel, to name just a few.

It's the same with lace and buttons; I'm attracted to white and natural colors. Whether lace is new or antique, I buy three to six yards of something that suits my taste and set it aside. I can then take it out whenever it matches the color or mood of an item I'm making. I buy notions and fabrics separately, but it's odd how often I find that they go together perfectly.

Plain fabric often seems to call for stamped patterns. I draw a pattern in my sketchbook and take it to a stationery

store to have a stamp made. Imprinting a design on an item, such as a drawstring bag, establishes its personality immediately. I enjoy applying different pressures to change the intensity of the pattern.

# COTTON

I believe that cotton is the most appealing fabric and most likely the first that comes to mind for most projects. Its abundant variety of weaves, textures, and colors from gaudy to chic provides countless choices to let you stretch your imagination.

You can enjoy this versatile fabric throughout the year, it has all kinds of everyday uses, and it's easy to wash. You will find everything from extremely soft, thin gauze to thick, sturdy sailcloth and denim. The technology that allows us to derive so many fabrics from one raw material is truly astounding.

I have definite favorites among the various types of cotton. I find cute flowered and checked patterns appealing, but I almost always choose white or natural fabric that lets me feel the essence of the cloth—something that has the plain, simple texture of the sheeting I used to see in my family's factory. This kind of fabric is always the starting point for my cotton projects.

# JUMPER

Instructions on page 78

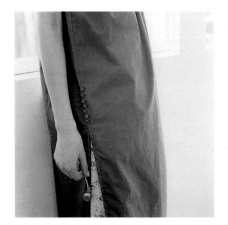

# JUMPER

This jumper has a roomy design so you can wear it anytime—by itself in summer or over a long-sleeved top in spring or fall. I've given it long side slits to give more freedom of movement.

## FINISHED MEASUREMENTS

Medium (45¾" long)

## MATERIALS

Cotton broadcloth: 35⅜" × about 118"
(The amount used will vary depending on the bust measurement.)
Covered buttons (⅜" in diameter): 7

## INSTRUCTIONS

❶ Using pattern paper, draw and cut out the front and back pieces for the yoke and the skirt (4 pieces), as shown under "Cutting the Fabric." (The B in the diagram indicates "bust measurement.")

❷ Make gathers (see page 110) along the seam allowance at the top edge of the skirt front. Pull the thread until the skirt top is the same length as the yoke bottom. Repeat the process for the skirt back.

## CUTTING THE FABRIC

Dimensions include the seam allowance. All seam allowances are ⅜" unless otherwise indicated in parentheses.

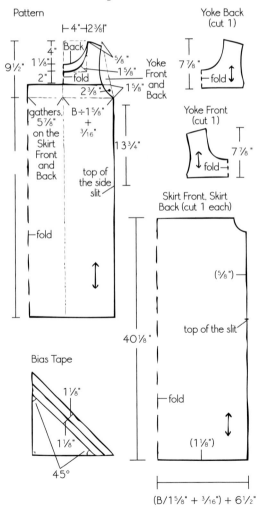

❸ Place the yoke front on the skirt front, right sides together. Align the raw edges and sew ⅜" from the edge. Finish the seam with a zigzag stitch or lockstitch. Press the seam allowance toward the yoke and topstitch along the bottom edge. Repeat for the back of the jumper.

❹ Zigzag or lockstitch the shoulder edges on the yoke front and back to prevent fraying. Place the front of the jumper on the back, right sides together. Align the edges and sew ⅜" from the edge along both shoulders. Press the seams open.

❺ Finish each armhole by placing the right side of the bias tape on the right side of the armhole, aligning the edges. Sew ⅜" from the edge along the armhole. Fold the bias tape to the wrong side of the jumper and edge stitch in place.

❻ Finish the neck by placing the right side of the bias tape on the right side of the jumper neck, aligning the edges. Sew ⅜" from the edge around the neck, stitching the ends of the bias tape together at the shoulder seam. Fold the bias tape to the wrong side of the jumper and edgestitch in place.

❼ Place the jumper wrong sides together. Align the edges and sew ⅜" from the edge down each side to the top of the side slit (13¾" from the armhole). Press the seams open and topstitch around the slits.

❽ Fold the bottom edges of the skirt ⅜" to the wrong side and press. Fold under another ¾", press again, and sew ⅝" from the edge across both bottom edges.

❾ Sew the buttons to the jumper along the seam just above the right side slit.

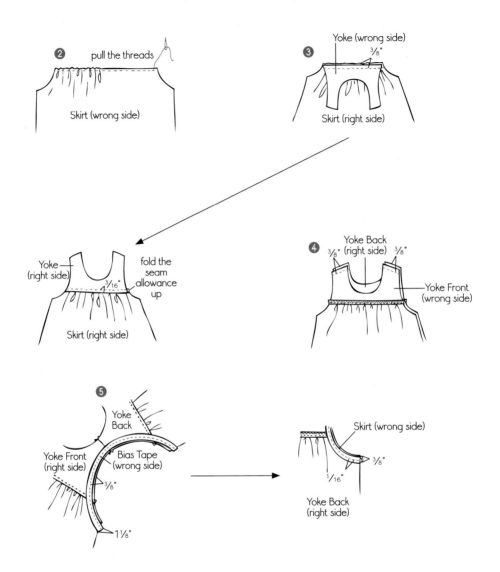

**2** pull the threads

Skirt (wrong side)

**3** Yoke (wrong side) 3/8"

Skirt (right side)

Yoke (right side)

fold the seam allowance up

3/16"

Skirt (right side)

**4** Yoke Back (right side) 3/8" 3/8"

Yoke Front (wrong side)

**5** Yoke Back

Yoke Front (right side)

Bias Tape (wrong side)

3/8"

1 1/8"

Skirt (wrong side)

3/8"

1/16"

Yoke Back (right side)

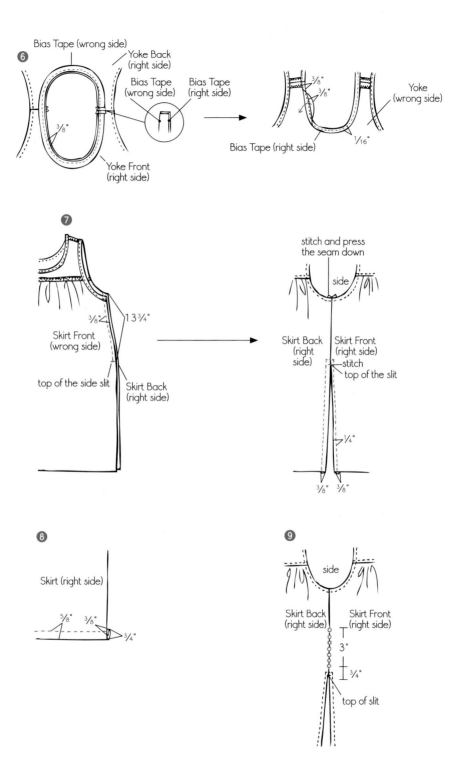

**6**

Bias Tape (wrong side)

Yoke Back (right side)

Bias Tape (wrong side)

Bias Tape (right side)

³⁄₈"

Yoke Front (right side)

³⁄₈"
³⁄₈"

Yoke (wrong side)

Bias Tape (right side)

¹⁄₁₆"

**7**

³⁄₈"   1 3¾"

Skirt Front (wrong side)

top of the side slit

Skirt Back (right side)

stitch and press the seam down

side

Skirt Back (right side)

Skirt Front (right side)

stitch
top of the slit

¼"

³⁄₈"  ³⁄₈"

**8**

Skirt (right side)

⁵⁄₈"   ³⁄₈"

¾"

**9**

side

Skirt Back (right side)

Skirt Front (right side)

3"

¾"

top of slit

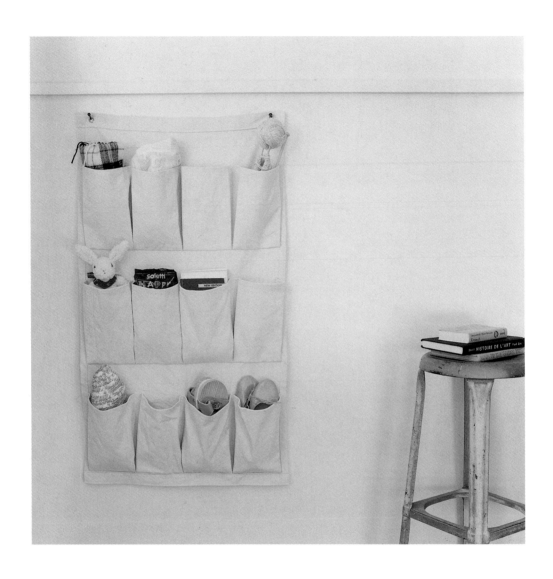

# HANGING POCKETS

Instructions on page 84

# FLOOR MAT

Instructions on page 86

# HANGING POCKETS

This multipurpose organizer is convenient for sorting small items in a closet or child's room. Take special care when making the gussets, which give the pockets their large capacity. I designed them to be easy-to-sew.

## FINISHED MEASUREMENTS

23½" × 40½"

## MATERIALS

Thick cotton (#10 sailcloth): 36⅝" × 85½"
Grommets (⁵⁄₁₆" in diameter): 2

## INSTRUCTIONS

❶ Fold one long side of the first pocket piece ⅜" to the wrong side and press. Fold under another ⅜", press again, and edgestitch. This forms the pocket tops.

❷ Mark the position of the pleats on the right side of the fabric. Working left to right, make the first pleat by folding the right pleat marking (2¾" from the edge of the fabric) to the left pleat marking (¾" from the edge of the fabric). Press and stitch in place ⅜" from

## CUTTING THE FABRIC

Dimensions include the seam allowance. All seam allowances are indicated in parentheses.

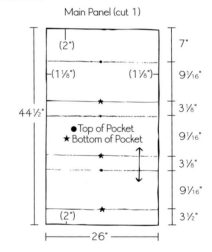

Main Panel (cut 1)

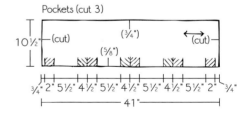

Pockets (cut 3)

the edge. For the next pleat, fold the two outside markings to meet in the middle. Press and stitch in place. Continue in this manner for all pleats.

❸ Place the pocket piece on the main panel, right sides together. Align the pocket 1⅛" in from each side of the panel, with the bottom edge 4⅛" from the bottom edge of the panel. Sew ⅝" from the edge across the bottom of the pocket.

❹ Fold the pocket piece up and arrange the shapes of the individual pleated pockets. Sew along the pleat centers to divide the compartments. Repeat steps 1 through 4 for the other two pockets, placing the pockets 3⅛" apart.

❺ Fold the side edges of the main panel ⅜" to the right side and press. Fold under another ¾" so the hem covers the side edges of the pockets. Press and edgestitch in place.

❻ Fold the top and bottom edges of the main panel ⅜" to the right side and press. Fold over another 1⅝", press again, and edgestitch. Set the grommets in the top edge, 1⅝" in from each side.

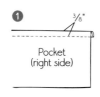

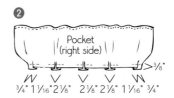

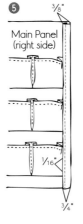

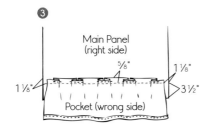

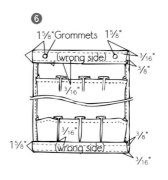

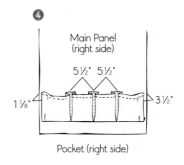

# FLOOR MAT

You can make this mat as large or as small as necessary, depending on whether you want to put it in the kitchen, bathroom, or entryway. I've used two layers of fabric to make it thick and sturdy.

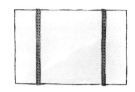

## FINISHED MEASUREMENTS

28¾" × 19¾"

## MATERIALS

Thick cotton: 59" × 20½"
Cotton tape (¾" wide): 41"

## INSTRUCTIONS

❶ Cut the cotton tape into two equal lengths of approximately 20½" each. With the top of the mat right side up, place the tape on the mat as shown in the diagram. Edgestitch along the long sides of the tape.

❷ Place the mat top on the mat bottom, right sides together. Align the edges and sew ⅜" from the edge along all four sides, leaving an opening of about 6" on one of the long sides.

❸ Turn the mat right side out. Fold the open edge ⅜" to the wrong side, press, and hand stitch the opening closed.

## CUTTING THE FABRIC

Dimensions include the seam allowance. All seam allowances are ⅜".

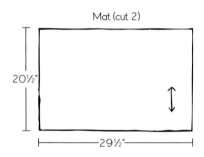

Mat (cut 2)

20½"

29½"

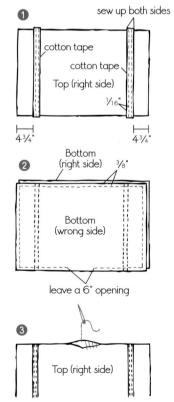

❶ sew up both sides
cotton tape
cotton tape
Top (right side)
1/16"
4¾"    4¾"

❷ Bottom (right side)   ⅜"
Bottom (wrong side)
leave a 6" opening

❸ Top (right side)

# SMALL BAG

I make a lot of drawstring bags to store miscellaneous items. I stamp numbers or letters on the bags to serve as labels.

## FINISHED MEASUREMENTS

6¾" × 8¾"

## MATERIALS

Gauze: 14" × 10¼"
Cotton cord (³⁄₁₆" wide): 19¾"
Embroidery floss: Red
Number stamp
Black stamp ink for textiles

## INSTRUCTIONS

1. Zigzag or lockstitch around the sides and bottom of the bag fabric to prevent fraying.
2. Fold the fabric in half, right sides together. Align the edges and sew ⅜" from the edge along the bottom and side, stopping 2¾" from the top.
3. Press open the entire side seam to the top of the bag. Edgestitch around the side opening.
4. Fold the top edge ⅜" to the wrong side and press. Fold under another ¾", press again, and edgestitch in place.
5. Pass the cord through the top hem. Stamp the bag with a number where desired, and embroider a line under the number, using two strands of embroidery floss.

## CUTTING THE FABRIC

Dimensions include the seam allowance. All seam allowances are ⅜" unless otherwise indicated in parentheses.

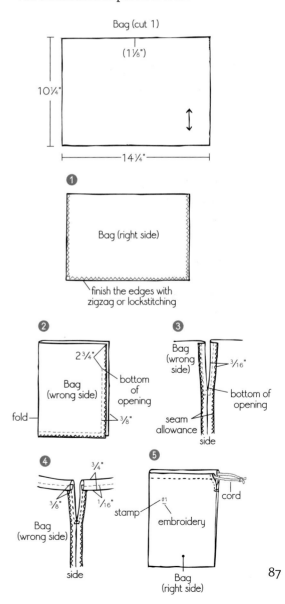

87

# SMALL BAG

Instructions on page 87

# SWEETS MAT

Instructions on page 90

# SWEETS MAT

Children always look forward to their afternoon snack, especially when it's served on a place mat to make it feel like a special occasion. I've added a little embroidery for color.

## FINISHED MEASUREMENTS

8" × 6"

## MATERIALS

Cotton flannel: 8¾" × 12⅜"
Embroidery floss: A color of your choice
Lace tape (³⁄₁₆" wide): About 28⅜"

## INSTRUCTIONS

❶ Embroider three French knots, as shown in the diagram, on the face of the place mat using four strands of floss for each knot.

❷ Fold the place mat fabric in half, right sides together. Align the edges and sew ⅜" from the edge along three sides, leaving a 2¾" opening on the long side. Turn the place mat right side out. Fold the open edge ⅜" to the wrong side, press, and hand stitch the opening closed. Press the seams.

❸ Lay lace tape around the edge of the mat and edgestitch in place. Fold the end of the lace under and hand stitch.

## CUTTING THE FABRIC

Dimensions include the seam allowance. All seam allowances are ⅜" unless otherwise indicated in parentheses.

Mat (cut 1)

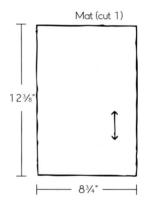

12⅜"

8¾"

**①**

(right side)

1 ⅛" $\frac{5}{8}$" $\frac{5}{8}$"

1 ⅝"

French knot

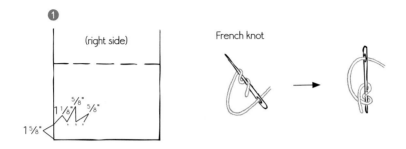

**②**

fold

(wrong side)   (right side)

³⁄₈"

leave a 2 ¾"opening

(right side)

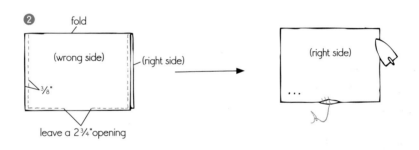

**③**

(right side)

¹⁄₁₆"

lace tape

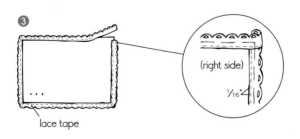

# LINGERIE CASE

Instructions on page 94

# LINGERIE CASE

I store all my lingerie and other small items for a trip in a bag like this. It almost makes packing fun, and the simple lace trim adds a feminine touch.

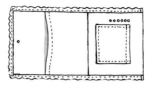

## FINISHED MEASUREMENTS

13⅜" × 27⅝" when open

## MATERIALS

Cotton flannel: 56" × 28¾"
Lace tape (¹¹⁄₁₆" wide): About 71"
Covered buttons (⅜" in diameter): 6
Snap (⅜" in diameter): 1 set

## INSTRUCTIONS

❶ Fold one long side of pocket A ⅜" to the wrong side and press. Fold under another ¾", press again, and edge stitch.

❷ Fold one long side of pocket B ⅜" to the wrong side and press. Fold under another ¾", press again, and edge stitch. This is the top edge. Fold the sides and bottom edge ⅜" to the wrong side and press. Place pocket B, right side up, on the right side of the main panel, aligning the bottom of the pocket 2⅜" above the panel's

## CUTTING THE FABRIC

Dimensions include the seam allowance. All seam allowances are ⅜" unless otherwise indicated in parentheses.

Main Panel (cut 1)

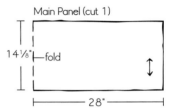

14⅛"  fold          28"

Pocket A (cut 1)

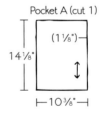

14⅛"   (1⅛")   10⅜"

Pocket B (cut 1)

9½"   (1⅛")   9½"

center fold. Topstitch around the bottom and both sides.

❸ Place pocket A on the main panel, right sides together and side edges aligned. Place the bottom edge of the pocket 1 ¼" above the bottom edge of Pocket B. Sew ⅜" from the edge along the bottom of pocket A. Fold the pocket up and align the side edges with those of the main panel.

❹ Sew the covered buttons onto the main panel, along the side of pocket B.

❺ Fold the main panel in half widthwise, right sides together. Align the edges and sew ⅜" from the edge along three sides, leaving a 4" opening along one short edge.

❻ Turn the case right side out and press the seams. Fold the edge of the opening ⅜" to the wrong side, press, and hand stitch the opening closed. Place lace along the top and both sides of the case and edgestitch in place. Cut off any excess lace.

❼ Center one end of the snap along the top edge of the case and sew it in place. Fold the case to determine the position of the other end of the snap and sew it in place.

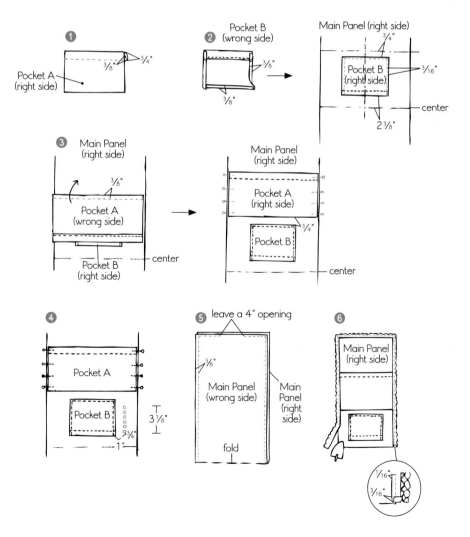

# LUNCH BAG

The handles are an extension of the main part of this bag, which you can use to easily tie the bag closed. The bag is also reversible. It's easier to assemble if you use a piece of thick fabric for one side and a piece of thin fabric for the other.

## FINISHED MEASUREMENTS

6" × 14⅛" × 4"

## MATERIALS

Cotton (solid): 10¾" × 29⅛"
Cotton (striped): 10¾" × 29⅛"

## INSTRUCTIONS

❶ Fold the solid fabric in half widthwise, right sides together. Align the edges and sew ⅜" from the edge along both sides. Repeat for the striped fabric, leaving a 2¾" opening on one side.

❷ Make gussets for each bag by folding each corner up where the fabric measures 4" in width. Stitch across the corner and trim the tip, leaving a ⅝" seam allowance.

❸ Press open the seams on both sides and cut away any protruding seam fabric at the top of the handles.

## CUTTING THE FABRIC

Dimensions include the seam allowance. All seam allowances are ⅜" unless otherwise indicated in parentheses.

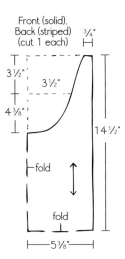

Front (solid), Back (striped) (cut 1 each)    ¾"

3½"

3½"

4⅜"

14½"

fold

fold

5⅜"

④ Place the solid bag, right sides together, inside the striped bag. Sew ⅜" from the edge all the way around the top. Trim the seam allowance to ³⁄₁₆".

Turn the bag right side out. Fold the edges of the opening in the striped fabric ⅜" to the wrong side, press, and hand stitch the opening closed.

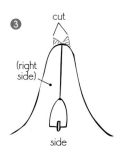

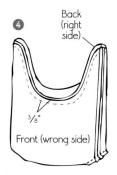

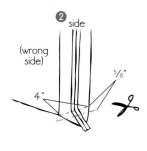

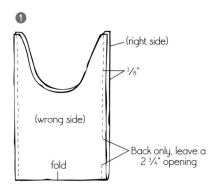

# LUNCH BAG

Instructions on page 96

# PARENT'S & CHILD'S BAGS

Instructions on page 100

# PARENT'S AND CHILD'S BAGS

You can carry these tote bags when you and your child go out together. Embellish each bag with a stamp. You can change the size and design of the stamp for each bag or stamp the same pattern on both.

## ADULT'S TOTE BAG

### FINISHED MEASUREMENTS

13⅜" × 15¾" × 4"

### MATERIALS

Cotton (#11 sailcloth): 26⅛" × 34"
Stamp with the pattern of your choice
Red stamp ink for use on fabric

### INSTRUCTIONS

❶ For each handle, fold the fabric in half lengthwise, right sides together. Align the edges and sew ⅜" from the edge along the three open sides, leaving a 3⅛" opening in the long side. Turn the handle right side out. Fold the edge of the opening ⅜" to the wrong side. Press the seams and topstitch ¼" from the edge along all four sides, closing the opening.

### CUTTING THE FABRIC

Dimensions include the seam allowance. All seam allowances are ⅜" unless otherwise indicated in parentheses.

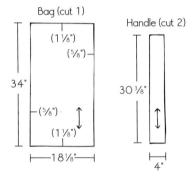

❷ Fold the bag fabric in half widthwise, wrong sides together. Align the edges and sew ³⁄₁₆" from the edge along both sides. Turn the bag inside out and sew again ⅜" from the edge along both sides.

❸ Make gussets by folding each corner up where the fabric measures 4" in width. Stitch the tips of the corners to the side seam allowance.

❹ Fold the top edge ⅝" to the wrong side and press. Fold under another ⅝", press again, and edgestitch. Turn the bag right side out.

❺ Topstitch ½" from the edge along the sides of the gussets.

❻ Place the handles on the right sides of the bag front and back, aligning the outside edge of each handle 3⅛" in from the bag sides and the bottom of the handle 3⅛" from the bag top. Edgestitch both handles to the bag.

❼ Stamp a design on the bag where desired.

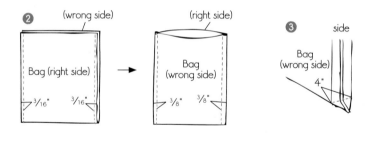

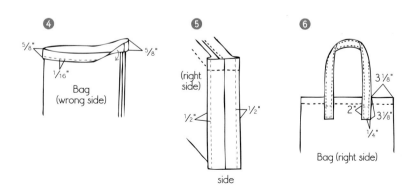

# CHILD'S SHOULDER BAG

## FINISHED MEASUREMENTS

9½" × 10" × 1⅜"

## MATERIALS

Thick cotton: 15¼" × 31½"
Stamp with the pattern of your choice
Red stamp ink for use on fabric

## INSTRUCTIONS

❶ Place the front of the bag and the gusset right sides together. Align the edges and sew ⅜" from the edge along the sides and bottom. Repeat for the back of the bag. Finish the edges of the fabric with a zigzag stitch or lockstitch.

❷ Fold the top edge of the bag ⅜" to the wrong side and press. Fold under another 1⅛", press again, and edgestitch. Turn the bag right side out.

❸ Fold the handle in half lengthwise, right sides together. Align the edges and sew ⅜" from the edge along the three open sides, leaving a 3⅛" opening in the long side. Turn the handle right side out. Fold the edge of the opening ⅜" to the wrong side

## CUTTING THE FABRIC

Dimensions include the seam allowance. All seam allowances are ⅜" unless otherwise indicated in parentheses.

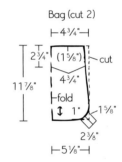

Bag (cut 2)

├─4¾"─┤

2¾" (1⅝") ⟋ cut

11⅞"

4¾"

fold

↕ 1"

1⅝"

2⅜"

├─5⅛"─┤

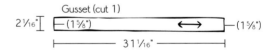

Handle (cut 1)

3⅛"

├────── 31½" ──────┤

Gusset (cut 1)

2¹⁄₁₆"

(1⅝")

(1⅝")

├────── 31¹⁄₁₆" ──────┤

and press. Topstitch ¹⁄₁₆" from the edge along all four sides, closing the opening.

④ Place the ends of the handle on the gusset, aligning each bottom edge of the handle approximately 2½" from the top of the bag. Edgestitch the handle to the gussets.

⑤ Topstitch ³⁄₁₆" from the edge all the way around the top of the bag, stitching over the handle on the sides.

⑥ Stamp a design on the bag where desired.

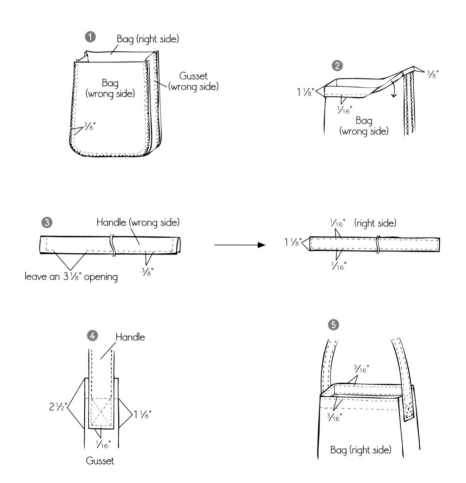

# ESSAY
## INSPIRATION FROM FOREIGN BOOKS

I'm attracted to things that have a foreign air about them, things I can't find in Japan. The first time I opened a Western decorating book I was transfixed by each of the interiors in the photographs. Even now, when I see bedrooms, bathrooms, kitchens, and living rooms, I think about the lives and daily routines that are carried out in them. I understand that people sleep in a certain kind of a bed, but what are their pillows like? What kind of sheets and pillowcases do they use? What kinds of towels do they use after their baths? What kinds of dish towels and aprons? I am especially fascinated by small every-day objects and accessories made of cloth. These items seem to contribute to the foreign atmosphere, and I experience a strange desire to create.

I also enjoy looking through picture books from other countries. Although designed for children, their illustrations are so detailed and carefully drawn that they are also interesting to adults. Again, I look at the everyday objects depicted, the rituals that take place at different times, the food on the table. The stories portrayed are usually unique, and the illustrators' use of color is often beautiful; I tend to get more involved in the world portrayed in the pictures than in the story itself. I enjoy looking at the patterns and designs of the clothing the

characters wear, trying to figure out the combination of colors, the sewing techniques, and the amount of fabric that would be needed to make them.

Picture books inspire my imagination more than photographs do. They not only serve as reference books for my handcrafts, but they also enrich my spirit.

# HOW TO CROSS-STITCH

First try embroidering your own initials. When you've mastered that, you can even embroider a slogan or other words.

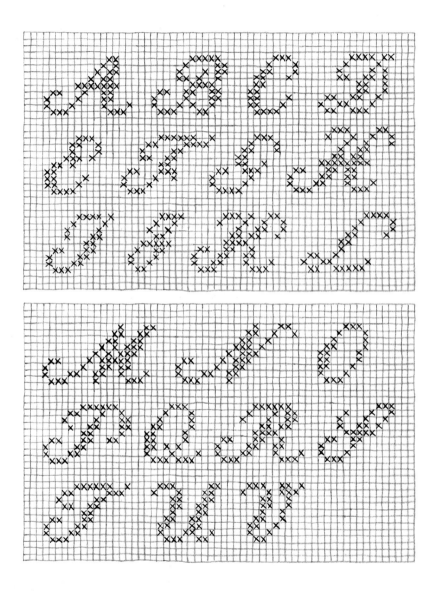

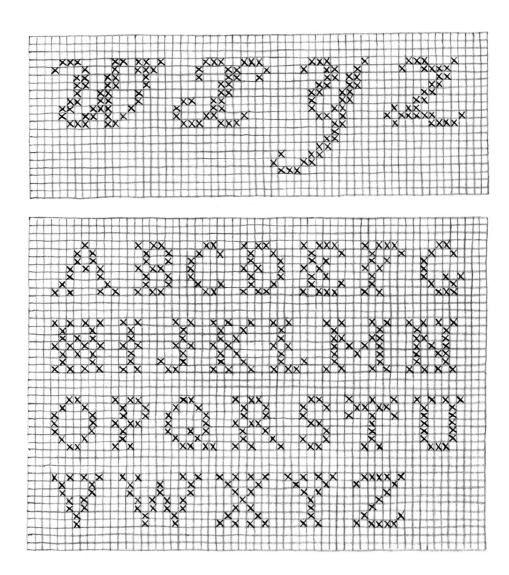

## CROSS-STITCH

Do not start with a waste knot, but leave a tail several inches long. Create an "X" by making two stitches that cross over each other, as shown in ❶ through ❹. Repeat this stitch to make letters and patterns. When you run out of thread, again, do not make a knot; instead, draw the thread end through the loop on the wrong side several times.

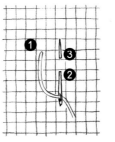
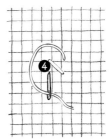

# NOTES ON SEWING

Here is a compendium of some little tricks that will help you finish your handwork attractively and tools that will make your work easier.

## USING WHAT YOU HAVE

When I was a child, my mother always used newspapers or handbills instead of regular sewing patterns to cut fabric. So I thought the term sewing pattern referred to newspapers or handbills—until I read instruction books and started sewing on my own. Of course, I don't use newspapers now, but perhaps due to my mother's influence, I hate marking patterns the way I'm supposed to. Instead, I pin a pattern to the fabric and make a few chalk marks here and there. When I sew, I use a magnetic seam guide to keep the lines straight, but I've never used chalk paper or a tracing wheel.

It may sound like a careless attitude, but if you're making something that you're going to use often, I don't think you should become obsessed with having everything just so. Just get started whenever you feel like it and see where the process takes you. You'll get more pleasure out of craftwork that way.

## GETTING READY TO SEW

### PREPARING FABRIC

Before sewing fabric, you should "treat" it to fix any irregularities in the grain and prevent it from shrinking when you apply a steam iron or launder it. Soak linen or cotton for an hour in water, then run it through the washing machine. Do this once if you only want to see how well it stands up to washing and twice if you want to bring out a special texture. Afterward, hang the fabric up to dry without squeezing any of the water out. When it is nearly dry, iron it with a dry iron on the wrong side.

Spray wool with water from an atomizer until it's moist, then press it lightly with a steam iron. When the fabric is dry, pull it to remove any irregularities in the grain. Check to see if one weft (horizontal) thread runs the full length of the cut edge. If not, make a cut in the side edge and pull out one horizontal thread. Iron the fabric to make sure that the warp (vertical) threads are at a right angle to the weft threads.

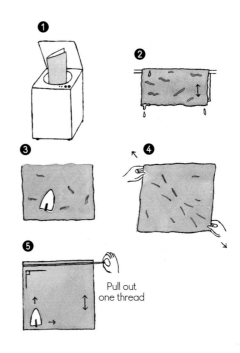

Pull out one thread

# IMPLEMENTS THAT I USE

## DRESSMAKER'S PINS

Use these pins to hold key points in place when joining two or more pieces of fabric. Line up the marks on each piece of cloth and insert the pins at right angles along the line you will be sewing. If you can't or don't like to sew with pins in place, or if you have to sew something that is several layers thick, baste the fabric in place with basting thread.

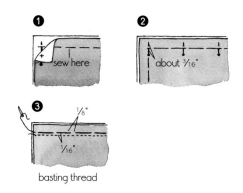

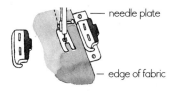

basting thread

## MAGNETIC SEAM GUIDE

Since I mark only the marking dots and a few other key points with chalk, I use a magnetic seam guide to ensure that I sew a straight line parallel to the edge of the fabric. I affix the guide to the needle plate of the sewing machine and run the edge of the cloth along the magnet as I sew. This lets me get by with less marking and reduces the risk of staining the fabric.

needle plate

edge of fabric

## PRICK PUNCH

When I'm sewing two or more layers of fabric with a sewing machine and holding the top layer in place with the machine's presser foot, the bottom layer may slide out of alignment to some extent. I use a sharpened prick punch to hold the bottom layer in place and feed it through. This implement is also convenient for sewing corners: when I sew a corner and turn the item right side out, I use the prick punch to push out the seam allowance.

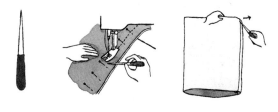

# HINTS FOR COMMONLY USED TECHNIQUES

## DOUBLE FOLDING

This means that you fold an edge twice to create three layers. If you iron each fold and create a firm crease ahead of time, the fabric will be easier to sew.

## Zigzag Stitching

When you stitch cut edges, lining the center of the zigzag stitch up with the edges of the fabric prevents the edges from rolling up when you sew. If you're using the zigzag for decorative stitching, you will need to use shorter stitches with narrower spaces between them. You change the thickness of the decorative stitch by adjusting its width.

Be sure to try this stitch out on some fabric remnants and practice modifying it. It will soon become one of your favorite stitches.

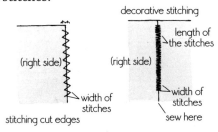

stitching cut edges

decorative stitching

length of the stitches

(right side)

width of stitches

sew here

## Gathers

Hand baste a row of large stitches about $\frac{1}{16}$" apart and parallel to the seam line. Pull the thread ends, sliding the fabric together until it is reduced to the desired width, being careful to keep the spacing of the gathers even.

Another method is to machine baste a row of stitches along the seam line. Do not backstitch at the beginning or end but allow the ends of the thread to remain loose. Pull the top threads to create the gathers.

For best results, if you're sewing gathered fabric together with ungathered fabric, use a prick punch to feed the fabric through the machine while adjusting the position and size of the gathers.

$\frac{1}{16}$"

seam line

pull

# RESOURCES

The fabrics and notions used throughout this book were supplied from a Japanese retailer, which you will find listed below. Since you may be unable to shop in Japan, retailers based in the United States are also provided, though they may not carry the exact materials found in this book.

GRAYLINE LINEN
260 West 39th Street
New York, NY 10018
(212) 391-4130
www.Graylinelinen.com

LINNET CO., LTD
Moriguchi Bldg. 1F
562 Kikuya-cho
Aneyakojidori, Tominokoji Nishiiru
Nakagyo-ku
Kyoto, Japan
+81-75-257-1128
www.Lin-net.com/English/shop_linnen.html

PURL PATCHWORK
147 Sullivan Street
New York, NY 10012
(212) 420-8798
www.Purlsoho.com

REPRODEPOT FABRICS
(413) 527-4047
www.Reprodepot.com
Online retailer based in Easthampton, Mass.

SUPERBUZZY
(805) 644-4143
www.Superbuzzy.com
Online retailer based in Ventura, Calif.

AKIKO MANO is the president of JAMJAM, a brand of handmade children's clothing and accessories. Her unpretentiously styled clothing, made with natural materials, has garnered a great deal of attention, and her creations are often featured at promotional events and in magazines. She lives in Japan.

TRUMPETER BOOKS
an imprint of Shambhala Publications, Inc.
Horticultural Hall
300 Massachusetts Avenue
Boston, Massachusetts 02115
www.shambhala.com

© 2005 by Akiko Mano, Chikyumaru
Translation © 2008 by Shambhala Publications, Inc.
Translation by Karen Sandness
Photographs by Chiemi Nakajima
Illustrations by Junko Raigo
Materials from Linnet Co., Ltd in Japan (lin-net.com/English/shop_linnen.html)

9 8 7 6 5 4 3 2 1

First English Edition
Originally published in Japan by Chikyumaru in 2005.

Printed in China

⊗This edition is printed on acid-free paper that meets the American National Standards Institute Z39.48 Standard.

Distributed in the United States by Random House, Inc., and in Canada by Random House of Canada Ltd

Library of Congress Cataloging-in-Publication Data

Mano, Akiko.
Linen, wool, cotton: 25 simple projects to sew with natural fabrics / Akiko Mano.
      p.   cm.—(Make good: Crafts + life)
Includes bibliographical references.
ISBN 978-1-59030-648-2 (pbk.: alk. paper)
1. House furnishings. 2. Machine sewing. I. Title.
TT387.M29 2009
646.2'1—dc22
2008031472